Learning Short-take®

STRATEGIC PERFORMANCE CONSULTING

Develop a proactive approach towards learning needs analysis

CATHERINE MATTISKE

TPC - The Performance Company Pty Ltd
Level 20, Darling Park
Tower 2, 201 Sussex Street,
Sydney NSW 2000
Australia

ACN 077 455 273
email: tpc@tpc.net.au
Website: www.catherinemattiske.com

© TPC – The Performance Company Pty Limited
First edition published in 2006
Second edition published in 2011
Third edition published in 2022

All rights reserved. Apart from any fair dealing for the purposes of study, research or review, as permitted under Australian copyright law, no part of this publication may be reproduced by any means without the written permission of the copyright owner. Every effort has been made to obtain permission relating to information reproduced in this publication.

The information in this publication is based on the current state of commercial and industry practice, applicable legislation, general law and the general circumstances as at the date of publication. No person shall rely on any of the contents of this publication and the publisher and the author expressly exclude all liability for direct and indirect loss suffered by any person resulting in any way from the use of or reliance on this publication or any part of it. Any options and advice are offered solely in pursuance of the author's and the publisher's intention to provide information, and have not been specifically sought.

For eBook version: By payment of the required fees, you have been granted the non-exclusive, non-transferable right to access and read the text of this e-book on screen. No part of this text may be reproduced, transmitted, downloaded, decompiled, reverse engineered, or stored in or introduced into any information storage retrieval system, in any form or by any means, whether the electronic or mechanical, now known or hereinafter invented, without the express permission of the author.

A catalogue record for this book is available from the National Library of Australia

National Library of Australia
Cataloguing-in-Publication data

Mattiske, Catherine
Strategic Performance Consulting: Develop a Proactive Approach Towards Learning Needs Analysis

ISBN 978-1-921547-11-9

1. Occupational training 2. Learning I. Title

370.113
___

Distributed by TPC - The Performance Company - www.catherinemattiske.com
For further information contact TPC - The Performance Company, Sydney Australia on +61 (02) 9555 1953.

HELLO.

Welcome to the Learning Short-take® process!

This Learning Short-take® is a bite sized learning package that aims to improve your skills and provide you with an opportunity for personal and professional development to achieve success in your role.

This Learning Short-take® combines self study with workplace activities in a unique learning system to keep you motivated and energized.
So let's get started!

Step 1:
What's inside?

- Learning Short-take®. This section contains all of the learning content and will guide you through the learning process.
- Learning Activities. You will be prompted to complete these as you read through.
- Learning Journal. This is a summary of your key learnings. Update it when prompted.
- Skill Development Action Plan. Learning is about taking action. This is your action plan where you'll plan how you will implement your learning.

Step 2:
Complete the Learning Short-take®

- Learning Short-takes® are best completed in a quiet environment that is free of distractions.
- Schedule time in your calendar to complete the Learning Short-take® and prioritize this time as an investment in your own professional development.
- Depending on the title, most participants complete the Learning Short-take® from 90 minutes to 2.5 hours.

Step 3:
Meet with your Manager/Coach

- Schedule a 30 minute meeting with your Manager or Coach.
- At this meeting share your completed Activities, Learning Journal and Skill Development Action Plan.
- Most importantly, discuss and agree on how you will implement your learning in your role.

GET VIP ACCESS TO YOUR MATERIALS

This Learning Short-take® includes an interactive activity book, associated tools and job aids, plus a bonus eBook.

1 Visit https://www.catherinemattiske.com/books

2 Select your book

3 Click: **VIP ACCESS**

4 Enter the code: SPC2022211

WELCOME

Strategic Performance Consulting
Develop a Proactive Approach Towards Learning Needs Analysis

Strategic Performance Consulting will provide you with key strategies to assist trainers, educators and facilitators to make a successful shift to the Strategic Performance Consulting (SPC) role and identify where you fit in this role.

The training function has evolved in recent years from a focus on training employees to improve individual performance, to a more comprehensive focus that aims to improve individual, team, and total organizational performance.

Trainers and facilitators are often asked to add strategic performance consultation to their existing roles increasing the need for effective and efficient activity planning.

Strategic Performance Consulting is a must for new or existing trainers, facilitators and educators who want to shift from a 'reactive training order taker' to a 'proactive learning business partner' and assist the organization in achieving its objectives. This Learning Short-take® addresses business challenges and traps and how to efficiently add SPC tasks into your role.

Strategic Performance Consulting includes the **Training vs. SPC Cycle Card**, and the **Strategic Performance Consulting Summary** and **Strategic Performance Consulting Flow** Job Aids, provided as a free downloadable tools.

Now let's get started!

1	Learning Short-take® > Start here
2	Learning Journal 73
3	Skill Development Action Plan 79
4	Quick Reference 85
5	Next Steps 105

"When a team outgrows individual performance and learns team confidence, excellence becomes a reality."

JOE PATERNO

"

"It is an immutable law in business that words are words, explanations are explanations, promises are promises but only performance is reality."

HAROLD S. GENEEN

"

Section 1

LEARNING SHORT-TAKE®

WHAT'S IN THIS LEARNING SHORT-TAKE®

Table of Contents

How to Complete Your Learning Short-take®	5
Activity Checklist	6
Learning Objectives	7
Let's Get Started	8
Part 1 - Exploring the Strategic Consulting Role	9
Part 2 - Strategic Performance Consultant Roles	21
Part 3 - 6 Traps for new Strategic Performance Consultants	27
Part 4 - Building Business Acumen	37
Part 5 - Managing Time	43
Part 6 - Strategic Performance Consulting Flow	55
Part 7 - In Summary	71

"The best performance improvement is the transition from the non-working state to the working state."

UNKNOWN

HOW TO COMPLETE YOUR LEARNING SHORT-TAKE®

1. **Reflect on your skills and abilities** in Strategic Performance Consulting and how you use this information to improve effectiveness in your role.

2. **Complete the Activities as directed**.

3. **Highlight specific skill areas** that you believe you could develop more. Add these to the Learning Journal as you proceed through the Learning Short-take®.

4. When you have completed this Learning Short-take® **meet with your Manager/Coach**. In this meeting, you will jointly establish a personal **Skill Development Action Plan**.

5. **Subject to your coach's final review** and assessment, you will either sign off the Learning Short-take®, or undertake further skill development as appropriate.

"The more you chase the Holy Grail of short-term performance, the less you get in long-term results"

WALTER CABOT

ACTIVITY CHECKLIST

"Let your performance do the thinking."

H. JACKSON BROWN, JR.

During this Learning Short-take® you will be prompted to complete the following activities:

- Activity 1 - Strategic Performance Consulting Initial Skills Self-Assessment — 18
- Activity 2 - Blending and Switching Roles — 25
- Activity 3 - 6 Strategic Performance Consulting Traps — 35
- Activity 4 - Business Challenges — 41
- Activity 5 - Time and Activity Breakdown — 46
- Activity 6 - Your Current Personal SPC Time Matrix — 52
- Activity 7 - Changing your Desired State — 53
- Activity 8 - Planning a Strategic Performance Consulting Project — 66
- Learning Journal — 73
- Skill Development Action Plan — 79

LEARNING OBJECTIVES

By the end of this Learning Short-take® you should be able to:

- Describe the Strategic Performance Consulting role and identify where you fit.
- List different Strategic Performance Consulting roles and how each SPC role relates to your role.
- Define six Strategic Performance Consulting traps and how to over come them.
- List critical business challenges and write how your role as a Strategic Performance Consultant can influence change.
- Analyze how your time is used currently and develop a plan of action to prioritize Strategic Performance Consulting projects.
- Create a three-step plan for managing a real-life Strategic Performance Consulting project.
- Create a Skill Development Action Plan.

"It is ridiculous for any man to criticize the works of another if he has not distinguished himself by his own performances"

JOSEPH ADDISON

LET'S GET STARTED

"How you measure the performance of your managers directly affects the way they act."

GUSTAVE FLAUBERT

The training function has evolved in recent years from a focus on training employees that aims to improve individual performance, to a more comprehensive focus that aims to improve individual, team, and total organizational performance.

Traditional training departments are under increasing pressure to make the transition from reactive service providers to proactive business partners, assisting the organization to achieve its objectives.

This Learning Short-take® will provide you with key strategies to assist you in making a successful shift to the Strategic Performance Consulting role and identify where you fit in this role. It will also enable you to clearly integrate learning and development aspirations within the broader organizational goals. This Learning Short-take® is designed for completion in approximately 90 minutes.

EXPLORING THE STRATEGIC CONSULTING ROLE

PART 1

PART 1 - FROM TRAINING TO STRATEGIC PERFORMANCE CONSULTING

Defining Strategic Performance Consulting

Strategic Performance Consulting is the integrated use of learning and other interventions for the purpose of improving performance, by addressing both individual and organizational needs.

The Strategic Performance Consultants Role

The Strategic Performance Consultant finds out how to identify where and why the organization is in need of performance improvement. Identify, select and recommend an intervention - not just training - that will bring about performance improvement. Then, measure the results of the interventions.

Specifically, the Strategic Performance Consultant analyzes and responds to individual, team and organizational performance issues and has many customers or stakeholders both inside and outside of the organization.

The Strategic Performance Consultant focuses on learning outcomes that are valued by the organization, typically measured in cost, quality, quantity, and timeliness.

The Strategic Performance Consultant works with a sponsoring internal client on a performance project.

The Strategic Performance Consultant's role is to help the internal client accurately identify performance issues and to develop the appropriate intervention.

Performance improvement interventions are aimed at the benefit of the whole organization, regardless of the internal client that the consultant is collaborating with on a particular project.

The sponsoring internal client may invite the services of the Strategic Performance Consultant to proactively influence a performance improvement project. **Training may be just one part of the performance improvement project.**

The Strategic Performance Consultant works closely with those who are formulating the long-term strategy and medium-term goals of the organization, and works at many levels in the organization simultaneously and brings measurable results to the organization's bottom line.

"The best way to inspire people to superior performance is to convince them by everything you do and by your everyday attitude that you are wholeheartedly supporting them."

HAROLD S. GENEEN

Defining Training

Training focuses on equipping individuals with the knowledge or skills they need to improve their performance to meet current job requirements.

Training is essentially a short term learning intervention designed for immediate performance improvement.

It is generally implemented for a variety of purposes, such as orientation for new employees, developing employees for improved job performance, cross-training, or to prepare employees for critical business projects.

The Trainers role

Trainers are involved primarily in face-to-face work with groups of people on courses, seminars or workshops.

Trainers use a range of methods for giving individuals the opportunity to acquire knowledge and skills for increasing effectiveness back at work.

Trainers are responsible to the training department for providing a service to the rest of the organization by reacting to customer needs.

Trainers also spend time in various administrative activities associated with conducting a series of training courses.

External vs. Internal Strategic Performance Consultants

External and Internal Strategic Performance Consultants share many characteristics. Both types of consultants help their clients address problems and improve business results. Both types of consultants have an internal drive for the expertise they bring to an organization and their ability to help clients solve business issues.

The roles of External and Internal Strategic Performance Consultants are similar in many ways, but Internal Strategic Performance Consulting is quite different. One difference is that the Internal Strategic Performance Consultant has a manager, on the inside! Also, some other differences are that they are often seen as staff serving other departments in their organization with complex expertise that is not easily learned by others. They may be trainers, career-development specialists, employee developers, performance improvement consultants, change management specialists or organizational development professionals, or other roles which include the duties of an Internal Strategic Performance Consultant as part of that role.

"The improvement of understanding is for two ends: first, our own increase of knowledge; secondly, to enable us to deliver that knowledge to others"

JOHN LOCKE

"The difference between performance and outperformance often comes down not to what you buy, but how you buy it."

JAMES CRAMER

Providing Vital Expertise

Internal Strategic Performance Consultants are valuable assets. They provide vital expertise to help their organizations meet the vision and goals. Successful Internal Strategic Performance Consultants bring a variety of positive attributes to their organization:

- Skills to analyze and design performance improvement strategies
- Expertise to train employees and help them develop necessary skills - or assign a professional trainer to do so
- Knowledge to align employees with the business strategy

External Strategic Performance Consultants work off site from their client organization and work more formally with an organization for either the whole or just a part of a project. Internal Strategic Performance Consultants have the opportunity to do daily and informal follow-up and to see a project through to it's completion over a long period of time.

Internal Strategic Performance Consultants do have a difficult role to play. They know their internal clients, their history, and their sensitivities.

Often these internal clients are colleagues and friends. These relationships are important assets when Internal Strategic Performance Consultants implement necessary organizational interventions.

Yet, these relationships can be the Internal Strategic Performance Consultant's Achilles heel if confidence or trust is damaged or lost, perhaps through an unintentional comment or a thoughtless act.

Maintaining objectivity and representing everyone in the organization is the mark of a successful Internal Strategic Performance Consultant.

"Limitations live only in our minds. But if we use our imaginations, our possibilities become limitless."

JAMIE PAOLINETTI

The Training Cycle

- Identifying training needs
- Setting training objectives
- Selecting methods of validation and evaluation
- Designing the training course
- Running the training course
- Carrying out validation and evaluation

The Strategic Performance Consulting Cycle

- Gaining entry into the internal business
- Agreeing a performance improvement contract
- Data collection, analysis and diagnosis
- Formulating proposals - learning and other interventions
- Feedback to internal clients and decision to act
- Implementation
- Follow-up

KEY DIFFERENCES BETWEEN TRAINING & STRATEGIC PERFORMANCE CONSULTING

FREE DOWNLOAD
To download this tool go to
https://www.catherinemattiske.com/books
and follow the online instructions

Complete Activity # 1
Strategic Performance Consulting
Initial Skills Self-Assessment

ACTIVITY 1: STRATEGIC PERFORMANCE CONSULTING INITIAL SKILLS SELF-ASSESSMENT

The following self assessment will give you an indication of your transition to Strategic Performance Consultant. Indicate the answer that best describes your behaviors currently as they are (not what you are hoping to achieve in the future).

		Never 1	Occasionally 2	Frequently 3	Always 4
1	I use both training and other learning interventions to assist internal clients with performance issues.				
2	I link learning outcomes with organizational business objectives.				
3	I proactively contact internal clients to discuss performance issues.				
4	I work with the business to help formulate both long-term strategy and short-term goals				
5	I use data to quantify learning and development initiatives.				
6	I partner with my internal clients to ensure a collaborative approach to identifying performance issues and agreeing solutions.				
7	I seek to uncover root causes for performance gaps.				
8	I apply business and industry knowledge to identify performance improvement opportunities.				
9	I use appropriate interpersonal styles and communication methods to build effective long term relationships with my internal clients.				
10	My internal clients trust and respect me.				

ACTIVITY 1: CONTINUED

		Never 1	Occasionally 2	Frequently 3	Always 4
11	I ensure adequate follow up and support to my internal clients following implementation of a learning intervention.				
12	I analyze and evaluate the effectiveness of learning and performance improvement strategies and make recommendations for future strategy.				
13	I am a team player who identifies and involves key stakeholders and decision makers for performance improvement projects.				
14	I effectively balance training design, delivery and administration with other aspects of the performance consulting role.				
15	I assist my clients to remove organizational barriers to performance.				
	Total (multiply each answer by the column heading (e.g. Never = 1)				

Activity 1 Analysis:

Whatever level you have achieved, it is important to remember there is always room for improvement. Identify your weakest areas, and focus on these when you come to your action planning.

15 - 30	30 - 45	45 - 60
Learn to develop your Strategic Performance Consulting skills and further expand your traditional training role.	You have reasonable skills for performance consulting; but there is opportunity to expand your role further.	You are an effective Strategic Performance Consultant. Use this Learning Short-take® to look for opportunities to further develop.

Now update your Learning Journal (page 73)

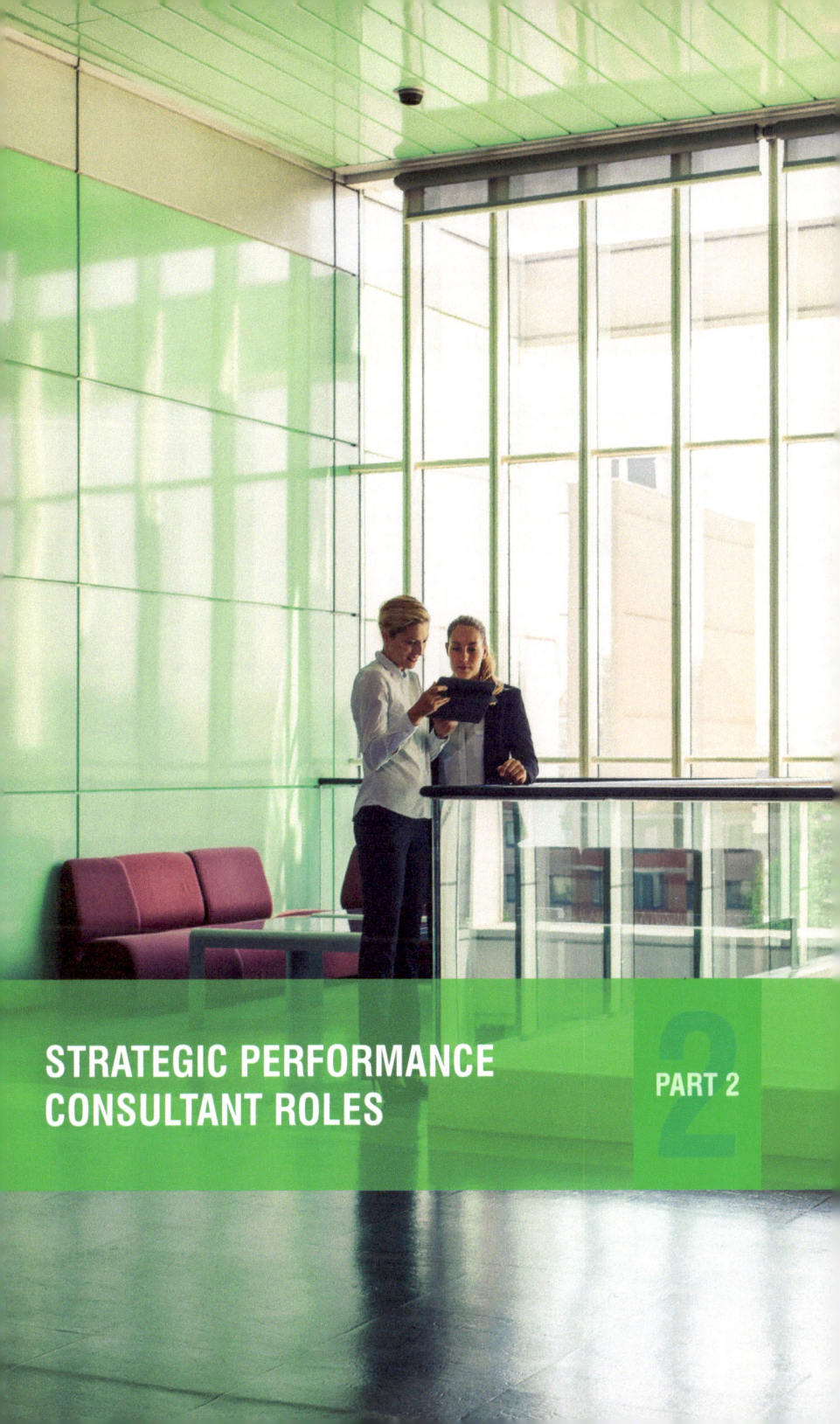
STRATEGIC PERFORMANCE CONSULTANT ROLES

PART 2

PART 2 - STRATEGIC PERFORMANCE CONSULTANT ROLES

There are many roles that an effective Strategic Performance Consultant has. If you are a corporate trainer moving into the role of an Strategic Performance Consultant you may need to sharpen your skills in simultaneously juggling many different projects and switching roles.

Blending and Switching Roles

The Strategic Performance Consultant role falls into four general areas:
1. Learning Strategist
2. Business Partner
3. Project Manager
4. Professional Specialist

Strategic Performance Consultant as a Learning Strategist

- Determines how workplace learning and performance improvement can best be leveraged to achieve long-term business success and add value to meet organizational needs.

- Leads in the planning and implementation of learning and performance improvement strategies to support the organization's strategic direction.

- Analyzes the effectiveness of learning and performance improvement strategies and makes recommendations for future strategies.

Strategic Performance Consultant as a Business Partner

- Applies business and industry knowledge to partner with the internal client in identifying workplace performance improvement opportunities.

- Evaluates possible solutions and recommends solutions that will positively impact performance.

- Gains internal client agreement and commitment to the proposed solutions and collaboratively develops an overall implementation strategy.

- Evaluates solutions against business performance.

- Uses appropriate interpersonal styles and communication methods to build effective long term relationships with the internal client.

Strategic Performance Consultant as a Project Manager

- Plans, resources and monitors the effective delivery of learning and performance solutions in a way that supports the overall business venture

- Communicates purpose

- Ensures effective execution of an implementation plan

- Removes barriers

- Ensures adequate support and follow up.

Strategic Performance Consultant as a Professional Specialist

- Designs, develops, delivers or evaluates learning and performance solutions.
- Maintains and applies an in-depth working knowledge in any one or more of the workplace learning and performance specialty areas of expertise, including: career development, talent management, coaching, designing or delivering learning solutions, improving human performance, leading organizational change and knowledge management.

"An acre of performance is worth a whole world of promise."

WILLIAM DEAN HOWELLS

Complete Activity # 2
Blending and Switching Roles

ACTIVITY 2: BLENDING AND SWITCHING ROLES

Given the four distinct Strategic Performance Consulting roles, answer the following questions.

1. What is the role that best describes your natural Strategic Performance Consulting Style?

    - [ ] Learning Strategist
    - [ ] Business Partner
    - [ ] Project Manager
    - [ ] Professional Specialist

2. For each role describe how you could incorporate this into your current role or how can I further develop this in my current role to be a more effective Strategic Performance Consultant.

	How I can incorporate this or further develop this in my current role	How would this increase my effectiveness as a Strategic Performance Consultant
Learning Strategist		
Business Partner		
Project Manager		
Professional Specialist		

As well as the four listed within the Learning Short-take®, identify any additional roles that you believe are important in Strategic Performance Consulting and explain why these are important.

Now update your Learning Journal (page 73)

© 2022, TPC - The Performance Company Pty Limited. All rights reserved.

"

"All of us perform better and more willingly when we know why we're doing what we have been told or asked to do."

ZIG ZIGLAR

"

6 TRAPS FOR NEW STRATEGIC PERFORMANCE CONSULTANTS

PART 3

PART 3 - TRAPS FOR NEW STRATEGIC PERFORMANCE CONSULTANTS

Trap 1: The Lone Ranger Syndrome

The tendency for many trainers is to take a training assignment and run with it. This is because trainers are considered specialists in designing and delivering training interventions. However, Strategic Performance Consulting requires partnership with the internal client and other stakeholders, because typically, some aspects of a performance improvement project will fall outside the authority and resources of the Strategic Performance Consultant.

A consistent short-coming with most new Strategic Performance Consultants is the failure to partner with key stakeholders in the organization. In addition, when they do try to partner; they often make the mistake of partnering with someone too low in the organization, or with someone who isn't the 'real' internal client - such as managers with whom the Strategic Performance Consultant already has a relationship. These people often aren't the ultimate decision makers.

Most performance improvement projects involve a number of causes and interventions that cross organizational boundaries and require buy-in from several teams or units. Partnering with the right players is important in gaining access and resources.

Successful Strategic Performance Consultants aren't lone rangers. They become team players who involve others, and identify key stakeholders and decision makers whose support is critical to the success of the performance project.

Trap 2: A rush to judgment

Internal clients are often in a hurry and tend to have unreasonable expectations of what the Strategic Performance Consultant can deliver. This is a particularly difficult challenge for new Strategic Performance Consultants who are keen to respond and act swiftly, often trying to get to the end of a performance improvement project too quickly. The process for improvement isn't always fast. **It is unlikely that a performance problem occurred overnight, so it is important not to try to solve it overnight.**

The tendency to rush to premature intervention leads to action before the Strategic Performance Consultant really knows what the problem is.

Failing to clearly identify the root cause of the problem means that the Strategic Performance Consultant may select an intervention that will not resolve the issue.

Successful Strategic Performance Consultants generate improved performance and that's possible only when root causes and key performance deficiencies are addressed.

Trap 3: Just-in-time = Too late

Too many new Strategic Performance Consultants take a reactive stance waiting for internal clients to contact them, problems in hand. Operating in this reactive mode, they forget that internal clients usually have a preferred solution in mind (most often training) by the time they contact the Strategic Performance Consultant. This is a missed opportunity to be strategic and go after performance problems that really matter to the organization.

A good Strategic Performance Consultant is a strategic partner and trusted advisor. This means that the consultant knows the internal client's business. It requires the Strategic Performance Consultant to identify emerging issues and be absolutely clear about what matters most to the organization strategically.

Successful Strategic Performance Consultants are proactive and anticipate problems that will emerge in pursuit of that strategy. The clearer Strategic Performance Consultant is about business goals and organizational strategy, the easier it is to be proactive and anticipate performance gaps.

Trap 4: No one's listening

Strategic Performance Consultants often become so excited about the possibilities around performance issues that they fail to see that the rest of the organization doesn't share their excitement. New Strategic Performance Consultants often expect that when they talk, their internal client will listen, often forgetting that they may not be the most credible source in the organization.

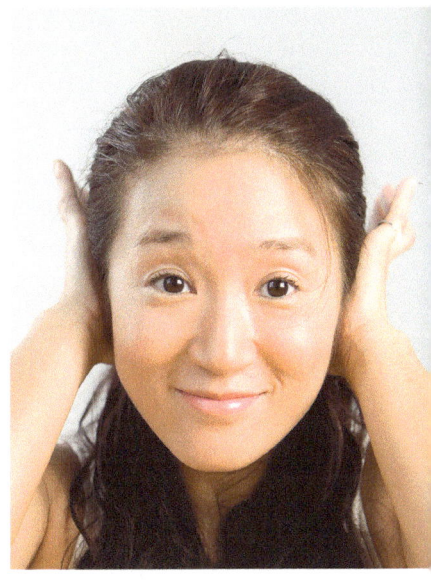

Often we develop new Strategic Performance Consulting structures in response to corporate demands for results, only to see internal clients continue to demand training, and ignore the broader range of Strategic Performance Consulting services.

Just because a Strategic Performance Consulting structure is established, doesn't mean that internal client's will embrace it or trust its judgment.

Successful Strategic Performance Consultants to build credibility through results and the provide good data to support their business proposals.

Trap 5: Prove them wrong

Internal clients frequently have their minds made up about what action they want to take prior to any discussion with the Strategic Performance Consultant. It may be a request for a specific type of training or team building.

New Strategic Performance Consultants often take the wrong tactic with internal clients and debate or even argue with them about solutions. This almost always fails.

Asking the right questions, pitching at the right level, and paraphrasing intent can move the internal clients from their original position so they invite the Strategic Performance Consultant to do a front-end needs analysis. This turns into a dialogue and exploration instead of a debate. With this approach the internal client is less likely to dig in his or her heels and insist on the original request. It also converts the consultant from an order taker or adversary to an advisor or even partner in solving the performance issue.

Successful Strategic Performance Consultants prevent this by becoming more proactive and becoming a partner and advisor.

Trap 6: Can't say no

A common mistake for many prospective Strategic Performance Consultants is to keep doing everything else they've previously done (all of the training, all of the facilitation, etc) and attempt to do performance consulting at the same time. This leads to the lament that there isn't enough time to do serious front-end analysis or evaluation work or the Strategic Performance Consultant role is unrealistic.

Moving to Strategic Performance Consultant not only involves a significant mind shift and approach to work, but also means saying no. It isn't possible to succeed at Strategic Performance Consulting by continuing to do what has always been done, and just add new work to the top of the pile.

The inability to say no demonstrates a failure to look at business goals. If there isn't a strong tie to important organizational goals, then the Strategic Performance Consultant will get occupied doing a lot of small projects that the internal client appreciates but that will have a poor return on investment.

All new Strategic Performance Consultants will face political realities in which saying no isn't a viable option, or there is a need to build trust and gain entry to the business. However, not saying no when it is called for can lead to work that contributes little to organizational priorities.

Successful Strategic Performance Consultants understand that just because there's a performance gap doesn't mean the work is worth doing. By identifying business goals and key performance drivers for those goals it is relatively easy to identify requests with low returns for the organization or no relevance to key organizational goals.

"When performance exceeds ambition, the overlap is called success"
CULLEN HIGHTOWER

Complete Activity # 3
6 Strategic Performance Consulting Traps

ACTIVITY 3: 6 STRATEGIC PERFORMANCE CONSULTING TRAPS

SPC Trap	Why does this trap occur?	How can you overcome this?
The Lone Ranger Syndrome		
A Rush to Judgment		
Just-in-time = Too Late		
No One's Listening		
Prove them Wrong		
Can't Say No		

Now update your Learning Journal (page 73)

FREE DOWNLOAD

Download the **Strategic Performance Consulting Summary Job Aid**
https://www.catherinemattiske.com/books
and follow the online instructions

> "Don't waste life in doubts and fears; spend yourself on the work before you, well assured that the right performance of this hour's duties will be the best preparation for the hours or ages that follow it."
>
> RALPH WALDO EMERSON

BUILDING BUSINESS ACUMEN

PART 4

PART 4 - BUILDING BUSINESS ACUMEN

Understanding the organizations business and financial goals

Business Acumen is the ability to:

- Understand the organization's business model and financial goals.

- Utilize economic, financial and organizational data to build the business case for investing in workplace learning and performance solutions.

- Align learning and development interventions with company strategy.

- Understand the mission of the business and develop learning interventions that facilitate accomplishment of the mission in an organized fashion when communicating with others.

"I think to really be an effective contributor, an Strategic Performance Consultant needs to understand the business and be able to think through the business's mission and objectives, and understand the systems that the business has in place to deliver its product or service, to really have a feel for what's needed in the organization."

ANON CEO

CEO Perceptions of the Six Most Important Business Challenges Faced by Organizations

The following challenges are six of the most important challenges faced by organizations today. Successful Strategic Performance Consultants consider the challenges that their organization is facing and proactively work to assist the organization overcome their challenges and align employees to meet organizational goals.

1. Financial Challenges

- Reducing operating costs to increase production efficiency.
- Developing and implementing business strategies that result in profitable return.
- Maintaining operating profits in an increasingly competitive business environment.

2. Recruiting Challenges

- Attracting and retaining an appropriate number of qualified and competent staff.
- Filling key positions.
- Improving current employees.

3. Technology and Internet Challenges

- Improving the use of technology to keep ahead of the competition.
- Gaining knowledge and employing those available technologies.
- Matching the latest technologies to customer requirements.

4. Globalization Challenges

- New employee skills to deal with a global economy.
- Cultural issues.
- New ways of doing business.

5. Customer Challenges

- Ability to partner with customers.
- Helping customers understand how to shop and buy.
- Developing technology for greater customer satisfaction.

6. Corporate Knowledge Challenges

- Shared understanding of the organization's objectives.
- Command of products and services to deepen customer relationships.
- Open communication and linkages between and among departments.

"Proper preparation prevents poor performance."

CHARLIE BATCH

Complete Activity # 4
Business Challenges

ACTIVITY 4: BUSINESS CHALLENGES

Use this worksheet to compare the business challenges your company is facing.

1. Add any business challenges that you see facing your organization that were not previously mentioned.
2. Then indicate your own level of perceived importance for you organization using the scale from 1 to 5.
3. State the specific challenge or challenges that your organization is facing
4. Finally, list some ways you think you, as a Strategic Performance Consultant, might deal with these business challenges.

(1 = Not Important, 2= Somewhat Important, 3 = Important, 4 = Very Important, 5 = Extremely Important)

Business Challenges	Your perceived level of importance	What is the specific challenge that your organization has	Ways that I can help my organization deal with the business challenges
Financial	1 2 3 4 5		
Recruiting	1 2 3 4 5		
Technology	1 2 3 4 5		

ACTIVITY 4: CONTINUED

Business Challenges	Your perceived level of importance	What is the specific challenge that your organization has	Ways that I can help my organization deal with the business challenges
Knowledge Management	1 2 3 4 5		
Globalization	1 2 3 4 5		
Customer Satisfaction	1 2 3 4 5		
Other:	1 2 3 4 5		
Other:	1 2 3 4 5		

Now update your Learning Journal (page 73)

© 2022, TPC - The Performance Company Pty Limited. All rights reserved.

MANAGING TIME

PART 5

PART 5 - MANAGING TIME

"The principle is competing against yourself. It's about self-improvement, about being better than you were the day before."

UNKNOWN

Many Strategic Performance Consultants also train and often undertake instructional design and/or training delivery. In this blended role, managing time is a critical skill.

For Strategic Performance Consultants who can work with others who write and deliver training, managing time is also a critical skill. Projects will be numerous and require simultaneous management. Most organizations have many priorities, often competing with one another for attention, which requires the successful Strategic Performance Consultant to manage expectations and juggle multiple projects.

Balancing Training Design and Delivery with other aspects of the Strategic Performance Consulting role requires time management skills.

Strategic Performance Consulting vs. Training

Training & Time

A series of training courses can be planned ahead in a logical manner, allowing time for preparation and other related activities. The workload for Trainers is often sequential, with a trainer conducting one course at a time, usually completing each assignment before starting the next.

Strategic Performance Consulting & Time

A Strategic Performance Consultant has to juggle several incomplete projects simultaneously. The workload is rarely sequential with multiple projects happening at one time. Timescales and commitments may need to be renegotiated as projects are extended, expanded into new areas or curtailed.

Calendar planning has to be flexible enough to cope with change and the unexpected. Above all, the consultant needs to be able to live permanently with 'work in progress' rather than the satisfaction of a series of finished assignments.

 **Complete Activity # 5**
Time and Activity Breakdown

ACTIVITY 5: TIME AND ACTIVITY BREAKDOWN

Looking at your present situation

Divide your working month into percentages (as a guide there are approximately 20 working days in each month i.e. 10% = 2 days).

1. Answering training requests from the business	
2. Handling training requests	
3. Proactively consulting and working with the business on learning and development opportunities	
4. Training (Face-to-face Physical or Virtual Classroom)	
5. Training (other)	
6. Developing training courses (instructional design)	
7. Administration	
8. Other	
Total	**100%**

Identify your top two most time consuming tasks. What factors contribute to this situation.

1

2

Now update your Learning Journal (page 73)

The Time Matrix

The Time Matrix was developed by Stephen Covey. In his book "7 Habits of Highly Effective People", Covey describes daily tasks in four quadrants. In the third habit "Put first things first", Covey suggests tasks are plotted on two axes: urgency and importance.

This model should help Strategic Performance Consultants prioritize projects and tasks ensuring that each task or project has a direct value to the organization and it's goals. Managing time on a daily basis using this approach helps Strategic Performance Consultants to work smart, avoid time wasters and maximize performance.

		Urgent		Not Urgent
Important	I	Crises Pressing problems Firefighting Major scrap and rework Deadline-driven projects	II	Prevention *Production capability* activities Relationship building Recognized new opportunities Planning *Re*-creation
Not Important	III	Interruptions Some calls Some mail Some reports Some meetings Proximate pressing matters Popular activities Some scrap & rework	IV	Trivia Busywork Some mail Some phone calls Time wasters Pleasant activities

The following table describes each of the quadrants and lists how we should or should not focus on each of the quadrants.

	Description	How we should attend to these tasks
Quadrant 1 - Urgent and important	Quadrant of Necessity	Manage
Quadrant 2 - Not Urgent and Important	Quadrant of Quality & Personal Leadership	Focus
Quadrant 3 - Urgent but Not Important	Quadrant of Deception	Avoid
Quadrant 4 - Not urgent and Not Important	Quadrant of Waste	Avoid

Put first things first

Why is it that some Strategic Performance Consultants seem able to easily accomplish their goals and make a difference in their organizations, but most struggle just to keep their heads above water? Wouldn't it be great if we could create two or three extra hours a day to finish an important project or make more personal time available? Maybe, but maybe not. This might only attack the symptoms of how we spend our time, and not really help us be more effective.

Putting first things first is not only about time management; it is really about "self-management". Putting first things first is practicing effective self-management, for "effective management is putting first things first."

Covey describes this as the fourth generation of time management. The maturing of time-management practices has evolved from:

1st Generation Time Management	Creating checklists and notes (first generation)
2nd Generation Time Management	Scheduling and calendaring (second generation)
3rd Generation Time Management	Prioritization that focuses on important work (third generation)
4th Generation Time Management	The realization that the term "time management" is a misnomer the issue is not to manage time, but to "manage ourselves"

"The first step to improvement, whether mental, moral, or religious, is to know ourselves - our weakness, errors, deficiencies, and sins, that, by divine grace, we may overcome and turn from them all"

TRYON EDWARDS

The focus of effective Strategic Performance Consultants is not to be efficient in how we do our activities, but to be effective in producing the right results.

Just as in medical care where the focus has shifted from emphasis on diagnosis and procedures to a focus on "outcomes," the focus of Strategic Performance Consultants must be on business results, not on activities (alone).

Mastering the Time Matrix

To master Habit 3, you must understand where you spend your time - and why it is spent there. The activities that always demand our attention first are those in Quadrant I, Important and Urgent. These activities include major projects with real deadlines or resolving crises that have harmful consequences if neglected.

The difference between effective people and others is that effective people know when things in Quadrant I are reactions to problems that could have been prevented and work to spend time in Quadrant II (Important but not Urgent) to prevent the problems from happening again.

To become proficient in Habit 3, we must analyze how much of our time is spent in each quadrant. Is our time driven by crisis management (QI), or are we spending time doing things to prevent crises (QII)? Do we have tasks that are not important yet seem urgent and often fill our days (QIII)? Or, have we burned out in fire fighting and crisis management to the point that we retreat into the escape of time-wasters in QIV?

If we never seem to have enough time for Quadrant II, then we must make time. We do this by eliminating things in Quadrant IV that are neither important nor urgent. Look at activities in Quadrant III that do not yield value. Challenge these activities.

Complete Activity # 6
Your Current Personal SPC Time Matrix

Complete Activity # 7
Changing your Desired State

ACTIVITY 6: YOUR CURRENT PERSONAL SPC TIME MATRIX

In the Time Matrix below, list activities that fit in each quadrant in the role of Strategic Performance Consultant that you CURRENTLY experience.

	Urgent	Not Urgent
Important	I	II
Not Important	III	IV

Reflect on each quadrant on your SPC Time Matrix

1. Reflect on the activities in Quadrant IV - how will you eliminate them?
2. Reflect on the activities in Quadrant III - how will you minimize them or even better, eliminate them?
3. Reflect on the activities in Quadrant II - how will you focus on these and maximize your time in this quadrant?
4. Reflect on activities in Quadrant I - how will you seek to be more proactive, so that these activities are not 'fighting fires' but simply important tasks that you can confidently handle urgently.

Now update your Learning Journal (page 73)

ACTIVITY 7: CHANGING YOUR DESIRED STATE

1. Reflect on Activity 5 & Activity 6.
2. Identify the 'desired state' for your role as Strategic Performance Consultant by reviewing and amending the time percentages from Activity 5.
3. List specific strategies for how you will achieve this change.

Activity	%	How I will achieve this…
Answering training requests from the business		
Handling training requests		
Proactively consulting and working with the business on learning and development opportunities		
Training (Face-to-face Physical or Virtual Classroom)		

ACTIVITY 7: CONTINUED

Activity	%	How I will achieve this…
Training (other)		
Developing training courses (instructional design)		
Administration		
Other:		
Other:		
Total	**100%**	

Now update your Learning Journal (page 73)

STRATEGIC PERFORMANCE CONSULTING FLOW

PART 6

PART 6 - STRATEGIC PERFORMANCE CONSULTING FLOW

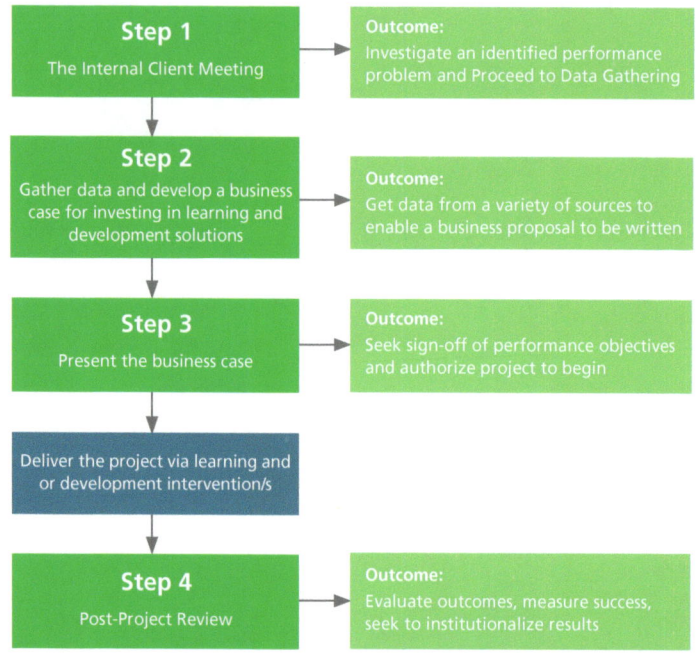

Download Job Aid of SPC Flow on page 95.

Step 1: The Internal Client Meeting

Critical to developing a business case for investing in learning and development is the initial client meeting. The purpose of this meeting is to investigate an identified performance problem. Typically this meeting will result from a client request, however the performance consultant may proactively initiate contact.

The client meeting provides an opportunity to clarify the original request for support, often a request for training, and restate it as a performance discussion.

Preparing for the meeting

The Strategic Performance Consultant prepares for the meeting by clearly identifying meeting objectives, preparing an agenda as a blueprint for accomplishing objectives, and gathering preliminary data.

General Flow of the meeting

The general flow of the meeting is to start with the internal client's request, then identify the performance gap and finally focus on root-cause data.

(i) Start with the client's request

- Assume that the request for training is in the belief that it will resolve a performance problem.
- Restate the request in performance terms.
- Help define the exact performance problem, the specific gap, and the causes of the gap.
- Prepare questions that will help define what performance is lacking and assist the client to see training as one of many potential performance solutions.

(ii) Identify the performance gap

- Often clients find it difficult to state the exact performance problem and to identify performance gaps. Instead they tend to go straight to preconceived notions about causes and solutions.
- Performance gaps are the differences between expected achievement and actual results. The gap may be categorized in quantitative or qualitative terms to provide a more complete picture of the opportunities available to improve performance.

- It is useful to undertake some research of performance gaps prior to the client meeting eg. audit and marketing reports, review of financial data, interviews with colleagues etc. This preparation enables you to ask the right questions.

(iii) Focus on root-cause data

- Influence the client to agree to collecting root-cause data. It will be difficult to close the performance gap unless hard evidence is collected on root causes and on the actions needed to provide a complete performance solution.

Detailed Flow for Initial Client Meeting

- **Define the problem** - clarify the internal client's request and perception of the performance problem.
- **Restate the request in performance terms.**
- **Identify the performance gap** in terms of expected and actual results.
- **Decide if the performance gap is manageable** and within your capabilities. If yes, proceed. If no, clarify with the client and reach agreement on the scope of the initiative.
- **Clarify your role** as a Strategic Performance Consultant and the client's role as co-owner of the data-collection process.
- **State the reasons and benefits of collecting evidence** on possible root causes of the gaps.
- **Discuss a high level plan** and time frame.
- **Gain client agreement** and commitment to the plan.
- **If necessary, schedule a meeting to review** and get approval of data collection plan.
- **Identify the resources** needed.
- Set date for the **next meeting.**

Now update your Learning Journal (page 73)

Step 2: Gather data and develop a business case for investing in learning and development solutions

The purpose of the Data Collection is to canvas and record input from various business sources in relation to an identified training need. Feedback from the relevant stakeholders ensures that the training content and process is appropriate for the needs of both the business and the employees.

Data Collection from People

Elements to be recorded

Record the conversations and meetings with people that you have contacted to assist you with the data collection process.

- Name, Position, Contact Details, Physical Location
- Status
  - For Example: Subject Matter Expert (SME), Business Sponsor (BSp), Target Audience Representative (TAR), High Performer (HP), or Reference Material (Ref).
- Indicate the date that the data was collected.
- Detail the data collected

Sample Questions

Sample questions that may be used to help with Data Collection from People

1. What do you think the problem is?
2. How would having this learning help you in your job?
3. Who else would you recommend I talk to?
4. What other resources would you recommend?

5. If the solution is likely to be solved by training:
   a. What do you think the training should look like?
   b. What do you see as the biggest obstacle that could prevent this training being successful?
   c. What comments do you have on course objectives and proposed duration of this training?
   d. What anecdotes do you have that we could use in class to illustrate a particular learning point?

Data Collection from Reference Material

Elements to be recorded

If it was Reference Material that was consulted for assistance with data collection (as opposed to a personal contact) you may wish to record the following:

- Reference Material source, title, author,
- Reference Material location
    - Provide details e.g. Internet URL, Book ISBN, Publication and Source Date, Other relevant information that would assist in locating the reference material in future.
- Indicate the date that the data was collected.
- Detail the data collected

Next Steps

1. Compile all data collected into a easy to read format. This process ensures that real business objectives are identified and approved prior to any training and development activity taking place.
2. Once the data has been collected and assessed, you will then be in a position to identify whether the project will go ahead. If so, the data collection process should also assist you in broadly shaping what the learning intervention will look like. It will also assist in determining if training is the appropriate learning intervention.

Now update your Learning Journal (page 73)

Step 3: Finalize the Agreement

This step ensures that all training development and implementation to be undertaken has been reviewed and approved by relevant parties, in line with business and performance objectives. This sign off is essential from your internal client.

The business case should very clearly identify the performance expectations on completion of the learning intervention and shows the results of the data collection into one coherent report for the business sponsor to sign off.

It is the final approval stage for instructional design and training logistics work to begin.

Determining the intervention types

After the data has been collected the Strategic Performance Consultant will need to recommend an intervention or a series of interventions to fill the performance gap or address the issue.

There are many ways of filling a performance gap. Interventions can be grouped in three ways: for individuals, teams and the entire organization. The following lists suggests some ideas for interventions in each group.

Interventions for individuals include:
- Coaching
- Education and Training
- Management
- Life and Career Planning
- Skills training
- Role negotiation

Interventions for teams and small groups include:
- Team development
- Leadership development
- Skills training
- Goal setting & Action Planning
- Workgroup learning
- Third-party facilitated learning sessions
- Responsibility charting
- Role negotiation

Interventions across organizations include:
- Process improvement redesign
- Performance improvement
- Organization restructuring
- Survey feedback
- Vision, strategy and culture alignment
- Large group interventions

The critical step

This step is the conclusion of the contract phase. It confirms the understanding by the internal client and the Strategic Performance Consultant about the needs of the client, the parameters of the project and clarifies expectations of what will be delivered, to whom and by when.

It's tempting to gloss over finalizing the agreement. This is especially true where the Strategic Performance Consultant and the internal client know each other and have worked together before. Each project brings different issues, roles and expectations. **Experienced Strategic Performance Consultants take the time to review the expectations, confirm each other's roles in the project and verify the actions that each will take to support the project.**

What goes in the Agreement?

A written agreement may often sound like a lot of work, but it doesn't need to be. Even an email confirmation, or minutes of meeting serve to keep the project on track and allow for a reference point throughout the project.

The agreement would include:

- **Background and Scope**
  - Description of the issue/opportunity
- **Desired Outcomes**
  - Summary of goals and tangible outcomes of the project
- **Summary of the data collected**
- **Summary of the Strategic Performance Consultants role**
- **Timeline**
  - List of key activities (interventions), timeframes and expected results
- **Logistics & Resources**
  - People involved, location, materials required
- **Communication Strategy**
  - Preferred communication method
  - List of key stakeholders and others who will receive information
- **Risks & Contingencies**
  - Known internal and external factors that may effect the project and contingencies for each risk.
- **Support**
  - Strategic Performance Consultants time commitment
  - Other necessary support mechanisms

The "Agreement" Meeting

Starting the conversation

A conversation beginning with words such as "let's talk about our expectations, what we are going to do, and how we will approach it" allows the Strategic Performance Consultant to avoid the more formal words of contract and agreement typically presented by external consultants.

Presenting the Proposal

Take the time to walk through the entire proposal with the internal client. Allow the internal client to ask questions and clarify the proposal along the way. A side-by-side meeting is often more effective than a formal presentation, however the level of formality will depend on the number of people attending the meeting.

As your role becomes more consultative, your credibility depends on how well you understand and make yourself understood.

Clarify Administrative Support

Often internal clients expect Strategic Performance Consultants to drive the project, provide the leadership, and do the administrative work. It's important for the Strategic Performance Consultant to clarify who will undertake the administrative responsibilities, such as arranging schedules, communicating with employees, entering data into a Learning Management System, and so on. This part of the conversation reminds people that the Strategic Performance Consultant is not always the 'hands on doer' but the overall project manager and change agent.

Staying true to the Agreement

Often there is pressure for the Strategic Performance Consultant to change the agreement once the project has begun, or to change the original brief effecting the value of the data collection. There is never a guarantee that key stakeholders will not make changes to the project, however the following ideas may minimize that from happening:

- Seek senior management buy-in and agreement to the proposal.
- Ensure that all key stakeholders are kept informed in key decisions.
- During the analysis phase discuss how other internal clients use your expertise.
- Resist pressure to take a different approach to avoid being accountable for less-than-successful results.
- Take time to address concerns and resistance.
- Involve other areas of the business that are impacted by the project.
- Plan communication processes. List who will receive project communication and how things will be communicated.
- List success criteria. From the inception of the project ask key stakeholders how they will measure success.
- Create an environment where open, honest and truthful feedback is acceptable and expected. Ask key stakeholders for this as a foundation stone to the assignment.

Complete Activity # 8
Planning a Strategic Performance Consulting Project

ACTIVITY 8: PLANNING A STRATEGIC PERFORMANCE CONSULTING PROJECT

Choose a real life project that you intend to begin working on. If you don't have an upcoming project, think proactively about a project that you could begin that would have a positive impact for the organization. (Refer to the 'Business Challenges' section of the Learning Short-take® to prompt ideas)

Reflect on the first three steps of the Strategic Performance Consulting Flow. Answer the following questions in relation to your **real life project.**

1. **Describe the project**

2. **Who are the key stakeholders**

3. **What is the aim of the project**

4. **Has the initial client meeting taken place?**

a. If yes - summarize the meeting outcome	b. If no
i. Was approval given for data collection?	ii. what do you need to do to plan for the meeting?
1. If yes, what is the scope of the data collection	
2. If no - how can you influence the key stakeholder of the project to give you this approval?	

ACTIVITY 8: CONTINUED

5. Has the data collection taken place?

a. If yes - summarize the outcome	b. If no - what do you need to do to collect the appropriate data?

6. Have you written a business case ready to present?

a. If yes - summarize your proposal (think about it as an 'elevator speech' - how would you describe your proposal in under 1 minute?)	b. If no - what will be your steps to prepare your presentation?

7. Have you presented your business case and have approval?

a. If yes - summarize the next steps	b. If no - what will be your steps to organize the presentation meeting and prepare your presentation?

Now update your Learning Journal (page 73)

Step 4 - Post-Project Review

This step focuses on evaluation and what has been learned as a result of the project. Evaluation may often bring uncertainty of process and expectation - people don't know what to measure, and how to measure it. Having straight-forward measures in places doesn't have to be time consuming, costly, or daunting. The outcomes of some interventions are difficult to measure, however choosing what to measure early in the project, that is realistic with the needs of the business, will make this step easier.

Evaluating the outcomes of Strategic Performance Consulting projects have a number of advantages:

- When projects have successful outcomes, senior leaders are more likely to support the investment in Strategic Performance Consulting.
- Lessons learned, both positive and negative, improve future projects.
- Feedback from internal clients, participants and other employees provide an opportunity for the Strategic Performance Consultant to improve their personal consulting skills.
- Credibility is enhanced.

Importantly, keep evaluation to results the internal client cares about.

How to discuss evaluation with the internal client

- Discuss how he or she will measure success of the intervention.
- Identify skills and behaviors that demonstrate change and ask how they'll be observed and measured.
- Measure what matters.
- Discuss the consequences of not measuring. Discuss measurement in terms of feedback to employees and high performance generally.
- Implement a Balanced Scorecard approach to measure the results of an organizational wide learning program.
- Seek out data that's already available (for example: sales results, customer satisfaction etc) and seek links to the learning intervention.

"You see things; and you say, 'Why?' But I dream things that never were; and I say, 'Why not?'"

GEORGE BERNARD SHAW

Post-Project Review Questions

Measure the internal client satisfaction with the project from the original brief to the ongoing project management beyond the learning intervention. Ask:

- What went well?
- What could have gone better?
- What would we do differently next time?

Now update your Learning Journal (page 73)

IN SUMMARY

PART 7

PART 7 - IN SUMMARY

"Consistency is the last refuge of the unimaginative."

OSCAR WILDE

1. The role of the Strategic Performance Consultant is very different to the role of a Trainer.
2. Focus on the organizational goals is of primary importance.
3. Link every project to organizational, team and individual goals.
4. Avoid the traps of Strategic Performance Consulting by working with key stakeholders, openly communicating, focusing on business needs and ensuring performance improvement.
5. Research the external influences of the business, business unit, team or individual.
6. Use the Time Matrix to plot daily tasks, focus on only important tasks and plan proactively to allow for time in Quadrant II.
7. Use the Strategic Performance Consulting meeting flow to keep projects on-track.

Section 2
LEARNING JOURNAL

The Learning Journal is used throughout the process to record your key learnings, hot tips and things to remember.

Update your Learning Journal at anytime. Ensure you complete your Learning Journal after you finish each activity. Then turn back to the Learning Short-take® to continue your learning.

LEARNING JOURNAL

As you work through this Learning Short-take®, make detailed notes on this page of the lessons you have learned and any useful skill areas. For each lesson or refresher point think about how you could further develop this skill. Your coach will want to discuss these with you in your Skill Development Action Planning meeting.

*"…that is what learning is.
You suddenly understand something you've understood all your life, but in a new way."*
DORIS LESSING

"Act as though it were impossible to fail."
WINSTON CHURCHILL

"The wise do at once what the fool does later."
BALTASAR GRACIAN (1601-58), SPANISH JESUIT PRIEST AND AUTHOR.

Learning or Idea	Action to be taken	Result Expected

Learning Journal - continued

Learning or Idea	Action to be taken	Result Expected

> *"Anyone who stops learning is old, whether at twenty or eighty."*
> HENRY FORD

Learning or Idea	Action to be taken	Result Expected

"
"Do not be too timid and squeamish about your actions. All life is an experiment. The more experiments you make the better. What if they are a little course, and you may get your coat soiled or torn? What if you do fail, and get fairly rolled in the dirt once or twice. Up again, you shall never be so afraid of a tumble."

RALPH WALDO EMERSON

"

Section 3

SKILL DEVELOPMENT ACTION PLAN

Your Skill Development Action Plan is the last Step in the process. After you have completed the Learning Short-take® and all Activities, update your Learning Journal, then complete this section.

SKILL DEVELOPMENT ACTION PLAN

This is the most important part of the program - your individual Skill Development Action Plan.

You need to complete this plan before meeting with your manager or prior to on-going coaching. You will discuss it in detail with your manager or coach as he or she will ensure that you have everything you need to complete the tasks and activities.

Once you have completed your **Skill Development Action Plan** schedule a meeting time with your manager or coach to review your plan. Take your Learning Short-take® and all other documentation received during the training course to this meeting.

Remember - you have committed to your **Skill Development Action Plan**, and need to make time to complete your tasks!

"The mind, once stretched by a new idea, never regains its original dimensions."
OLIVER WENDELL HOLMES

"Whatever you can do or dream you can - begin it. Boldness has genius, power and magic."
JOHANN WOLFGANG VON GOETHE

"Imagination is the eye of the soul."
JOSEPH JOUBERT (1754-1824)

Task or activity (Be specific)	Measure (this will help you to know you have achieved it)	Date (Be specific)
Reflect on your Learning Journal. Transfer action items that you can apply to your job. Ensure that you include some 'stretch goals' and also a blend of short, medium and long term goals.	Apart from you, who else is needed to assist you in achieving your goal.	Be specific. A general date such as 'Quarter 1', 'August', or 'by end of year' is vague and more likely to result in not achieving your target. Be specific – e.g. 22nd November.

IDEAS FOR DISCUSSION WITH MY MANAGER

Ideas

CONGRATULATIONS!

You've now completed this Learning Short-take®.

Meet with your Manager/Coach to discuss your
Skill Development Action Plan.

Suggested Readings

- Mark Thomas (1996) **High-Performance Consulting Skills: The Internal Consultant's Guide to Value-Added Performance**
- Dana Gains Robinson & James Robinson (1996) **Performance Consulting**
- Worthen, Blaine R, James R. Sanders, Jody L. Fitzpatrick (1997). **Program Evaluation: Alternative Approaches and Practical Guidelines** (Second Edition).Addison, Wesley, Longman, Inc.
- Sieloff, Debra A. (1999). **The Bridge Evaluation Model.** International Society for Performance Improvement.

QUICK REFERENCE

This Quick Reference provides you with a summary of key concepts, models and reference material from Learning Short-takes®. We have also included some quotations to ponder.

Use this section as a quick reference to keep your learning active.

Quick Reference

Defining Strategic Performance Consulting

Strategic Performance Consulting is the integrated use of learning and other interventions for the purpose of improving performance, by addressing both individual and organizational needs.

The Performance Consulting Cycle

1. Gaining entry into the internal business
2. Agreeing a performance improvement contract
3. Data collection, analysis and diagnosis
4. Formulating proposals - learning and other interventions
5. Feedback to internal clients and decision to act
6. Implementation
7. Follow-up

Quick Reference

> **An acre of performance is worth a whole world of promise.**
>
> William Dean Howells

Blending and Switching Roles

1. Learning Strategist
2. Business Partner
3. Project Manager
4. Professional Specialist

Quick Reference

Traps for new Strategic Performance Consultants

Trap 1: The Lone Ranger Syndrome

Trap 2: A rush to judgment

Trap 3: Just-in-time = Too late

Trap 4: No one's listening

Trap 5: Prove them wrong

Trap 6: Can't say no

CEO Perceptions of the Six Most Important Business Challenges Faced by Organizations

1. Financial Challenges
2. Recruiting Challenges
3. Technology and Internet Challenges
4. Globalization Challenges
5. Customer Challenges
6. Corporate Knowledge Challenges

Quick Reference

The Time Matrix

	Urgent	**Not Urgent**
Important	**I** Crises Pressing problems Firefighting Major scrap and rework Deadline-driven projects	**II** Prevention *Production capability* activities Relationship building Recognized new opportunities Planning *Re*-creation
Not Important	**III** Interruptions Some calls Some mail Some reports Some meetings Proximate pressing matters Popular activities Some scrap & rework	**IV** Trivia Busywork Some mail Some phone calls Time wasters Pleasant activities

Put first things first

Putting first things first is not only about time management; it is really about "self-management". Putting first things first is practicing effective self-management, for "effective management is putting first things first."

Quick Reference

> **The more you chase the Holy Grail of short term performance, the less you get in long-term results.**
>
> Walter Cabot

Strategic Performance Consulting Flow

Step 1 - The Internal Client Meeting
Outcome: Investigate an identified performance problem and Proceed to Data Gathering

Step 2 - Gather data and develop a business case for investing in learning and development solutions
Outcome: Get data from a variety of sources to enable a business proposal to be written

Step 3 - Present the business case
Outcome: Seek sign-off of performance objectives and authorize project to begin

Deliver the project via learning and or development intervention/s

Step 4 - Post-Project Review
Outcome: Evaluate outcomes, measure success, seek to institutionalize results

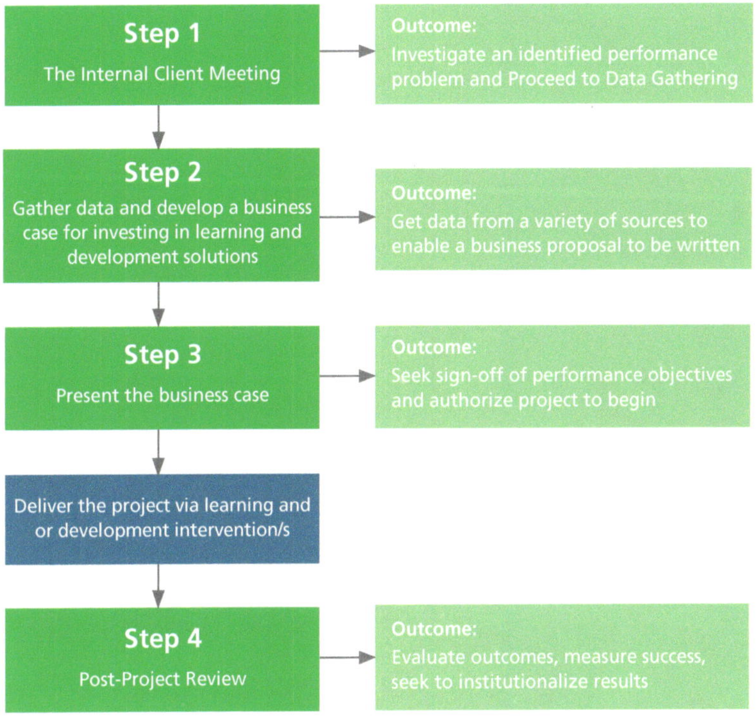

FREE DOWNLOAD
Download the **Strategic Performance Consulting Flow** Job Aid
https://www.catherinemattiske.com/books
and follow the online instructions

Quick Reference

Step 1:
The Internal Client Meeting

General Flow for Initial Client Meeting

1. Start with the client's request

2. Identify the performance gap

3. Focus on root-cause data

Step 1: The Internal Client Meeting

Detailed Flow for Initial Client Meeting

1. Define the problem
2. Restate the request in performance terms
3. Identify the performance gap
4. Decide if the performance gap is manageable
5. Clarify your role
6. State the reasons and benefits of collecting evidence
7. Discuss a high level plan
8. Gain client agreement
9. If necessary, schedule a meeting to review
10. Identify the resources
11. Set date for the next meeting.

Quick Reference

Step 2: Gather data and develop a business case for investing in learning and development solutions

The purpose of the Data Collection is to canvas and record input from various business sources in relation to an identified training need. Feedback from the relevant stakeholders ensures that the training content and process is appropriate for the needs of both the business and the employees.

Data Collection from People

Sample Questions

1. What do you think the problem is?
2. How would having this learning help you in your job?
3. Who else would you recommend I talk to?
4. What other resources would you recommend?
5. If the solution is likely to be solved by training:
    a. What do you think the training should look like?
    b. What do you see as the biggest obstacle that could prevent this training being successful?
    c. What comments do you have on course objectives and proposed duration of this training?
    d. What anecdotes do you have that we could use in class to illustrate a particular learning point?

Quick Reference

Data Collection from Reference Material

Elements to be recorded

- Reference Material source, title and author
- Reference Material location
- Indicate the date that the data was collected
- Detail the data collected.

Step 3: Finalize the Agreement

The business case should very clearly identify the performance expectations on completion of the learning intervention and shows the results of the data collection into one coherent report for the business sponsor to sign off.

Quick Reference

Intervention Types

Individuals
- Coaching
- Education and Training
- Management
- Life and Career Planning
- Skills training
- Role negotiation

Teams and Small Groups
- Team development
- Leadership development
- Skills training
- Goal setting & Action Planning
- Workgroup learning
- Third-party facilitated learning sessions
- Responsibility charting
- Role negotiation

Organizations
- Process improvement redesign
- Performance improvement
- Organization restructuring
- Survey feedback
- Vision, strategy and culture alignment
- Large group interventions

Step 4: Post-Project Review

Focus on evaluation and what has been learned as a result of the project. Having straight-forward measures in places doesn't have to be time consuming, costly, or daunting.

Discuss evaluation with the internal client: How will they measure success?

Measure the internal client satisfaction with the project. Ask:

- What went well?
- What could have gone better?
- What would we do differently next time?

"

"Don't lower your expectations to meet your performance. Raise your level of performance to meet your expectations. Expect the best of yourself, and then do what is necessary to make it a reality."

RALPH MARSTON

"

NEXT STEPS

Congratulations! You have now completed this Learning Short-take® title. The entire list of Learning Short-takes® can be found on the catherinemattiske.com website.

In this section we have suggested Learning Short-take® titles for you that will build your learning. You may order these Learning Short-takes® online at https://www.catherinemattiske.com/books or from your bookstores.

Influencing for Opportunity
Identify and Maximize Ways to Influence

Course Content

- Part 1: Fundamentals of Influence
- Part 2: Influence: A Choice
- Part 3: Naturally Occurring Influence Patterns
- Part 4: Methods of Persuasion
- Part 5: The Challenges of Influence
- Part 6: Building a life of Influence

Learning Short-take® Outline

Influencing for Opportunity combines self-study with realistic workplace activities to provide you with the key skills and techniques to influence those around you. You will learn the theory of influence, influence principles and strategies, as well as how to plan and prepare for important opportunities to influence. As a result, you should achieve greater results in your organization, work more productively and effectively in a team environment, and develop stronger working relationships with co-workers, suppliers and customers.

The ability to influence others is critical in today's competitive business environment. Being highly skilled in influence enables you to build the relationships you need to get results inside or outside the organization. Employees and managers alike cannot assume they have power over others - they must earn it through influence. Being an influential person is a skill that can be learned and practiced. **Influencing for Opportunity** will help you succeed in the modern corporate environment by increasing your ability to influence others.

Influencing for Opportunity includes a **toolkit of job aids and learning support tools** provided to you as free downloads.

Learning Objectives

- Identify patterns of influence.
- Evaluate how you currently use influence behaviors and identify areas for development.
- Develop influence behaviors for greater personal and business success.
- Establish clear and powerful influence goals.
- Increase influence to overcome resistance.
- Describe how to ask for and receive support.
- Design an approach for formal and informal influence situations; apply the approach to a real-life situation.
- Create a Skill Development Action Plan.

Adult Learning Principles 1
Understanding the Ways Adults Learn

Learning Short-take® Outline

Adult Learning Principles 1 combines self-study with realistic workplace activities for trainers, educators, facilitators and managers to develop skills and knowledge in the principles of adult learning. It will add adult learning techniques to your 'grab bag' of learning design tools for improved learning outcomes. After evaluation of your current approach to learning design, you will learn to develop new and innovative strategies to engage learners at every level. Significantly increasing participant retention and training results **Adult Learning Principles 1** will fuel your confidence in designing successful training workshops and eLearning every time.

The principles of adult learning work on the basis that we all learn differently, and the way we like to receive and interpret information varies from person to person. Trainers and facilitators who use a combination of adult learning principles to provide balance in their programs increase the chances of keeping all participants focused and engaged throughout the learning process. **Adult Learning Principles 1** will assist you in building a good mix of adult learning styles which is critical in ensuring learning, thorough participant retention and workplace application.

Adult Learning Principles 1 includes the job aid Strategies for Meeting Global and Specific Needs, the **Adult Learning Principles Quick Reference Wall Chart** and the **Activity Booklet**, provided as free downloadable tools.

Course Content

- Part 1: Understanding Adult Learners
- Part 2: Adult Learning Principle 1 - Global vs Specific Learners
- Part 3: Adult Learning Principle 2 - Learning Style - Modalities
- Part 4: Adult Learning Principle 3 - Learning Types - The 4Mat System

Learning Objectives

- Successfully match adult learning terms with definitions.
- Determine your personal Learning Style preference.
- List and give working examples of three Adult Learning Principles – Global vs Specific, Learning Styles and Learning Types.
- Develop strategies and ideas to link Adult Learning Principles with Instructional Design.

Effective Time Management
Clear the Clutter and Focus on What's Important

Course Content

- Part 1: Getting Started
- Part 2: Time Matrix
- Part 3: Daily and Weekly Actions
- Part 4: Tips and Traps
- Part 5: A Final Thought

Learning Short-take® Outline

Effective Time Management combines self-study with realistic workplace activities to provide the key skills and techniques that allow you to manage your time more effectively. You will learn to do the things you 'have to do' more efficiently, and generate more time for the things you 'want to do'. You will learn tips, tricks and techniques to ensure a positive return on your investment in time, increasing success in both your work and personal life.

Time is our most unique and valuable resource. We all have 24 hours in a day, 168 hours in a week, and we spend it at the same rate. Time management is about more than time - it is really about managing our lives. **Effective Time Management** will assist you to balance priorities, achieve more, be more efficient and learn to maximize minutes!

Effective Time Management includes the **Daily To Do List** and the **Weekly Planner**, provided to you as free downloadable tools.

Learning Objectives

- Identify your own habits and time management behavior.
- Set short, medium and long term goals.
- Weed out tasks that are unimportant or a waste of time.
- Prioritize your work and create daily and weekly planners.
- Make instant changes to your workspace.
- Handle interruptions and avoid sidetracks.

www.catherinemattiske.com

www.ingramcontent.com/pod-product-compliance
Lightning Source LLC
Chambersburg PA
CBHW042230090526
44587CB00001B/14